ZOOM In on Animals!

Great White Sharks

Up Close

Carmen Bredeson

Enslow Elementary

CONTENTS

WORDS TO KNOW

cartilage (KAR tih lehj)—Hard, rubber-like material inside the body of a person or animal.

gills—What animals use for breathing under the water.

oxygen (AHK sih jehn)—A gas that animals and humans breathe.

skeleton (SKEL eh tuhn)—The bones or cartilage in animal and human bodies. It helps give the body shape.

veins (vaynz)—Tubes that carry blood in the body.

Parts of a Great White Shark

tail

fin

gill slits

mouth

eye

nose

GREAT WHITE SHARKS

Great white sharks live
in oceans all over the
world. They are the biggest
meat-eating sharks.

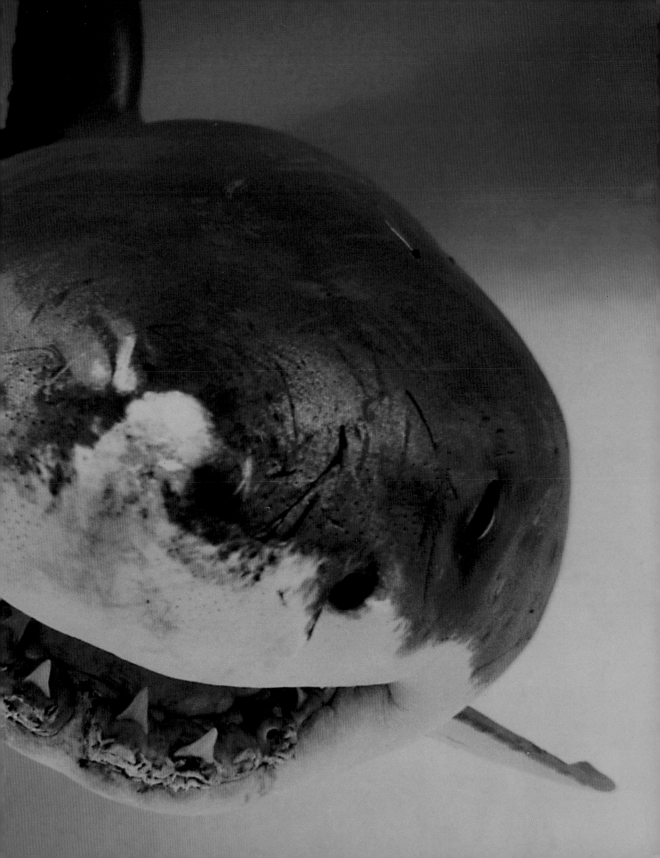

SHARK TEETH

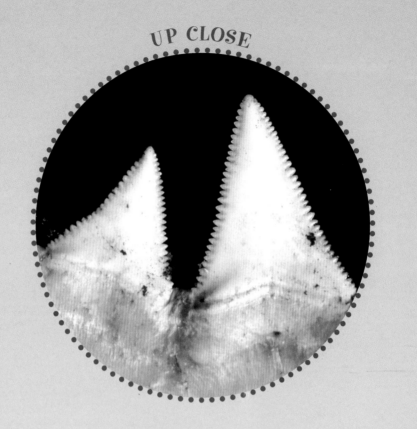

Rows of huge, sharp teeth fill the shark's mouth. When a tooth wears out, another one moves into its place. Great whites do not chew their food. They bite off big chunks and swallow them whole.

SHARK FOOD

UP CLOSE

green
sea turtle

Great white sharks will eat almost anything.
Seals, sea lions, turtles, and birds are favorite
meals. So are tuna, dolphins, and small whales.
Great white sharks will even eat baby sharks.

SHARK EYES

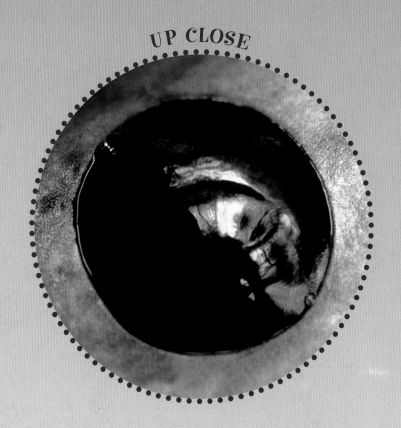

UP CLOSE

A great white shark can hold its head out of water. Its big, black eyes look for food. *Chomp!* The shark bites. Its eyes roll back in its head. This protects the shark's eyes during a fight.

SHARK SKIN

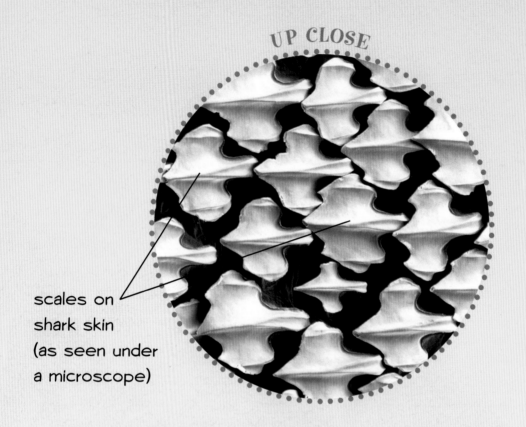

UP CLOSE

scales on
shark skin
(as seen under
a microscope)

Great whites have gray and white skin.
The skin feels bumpy, like sandpaper.

Great white sharks do not have bones.
A shark's skeleton is made of cartilage.
Cartilage is what makes your nose and ears
stiff. It does not weigh as much as bone.

12

Great whites can swim fast because
they do not have heavy bones. Their
scales help them swim fast too.

SHARK TAIL

A great white's tail moves back and forth.
The tail pushes the shark through the water.
The faster the tail moves, the faster the
shark swims.

SHARK FINS

Fins help a shark move. A tall fin on its back keeps the shark moving straight. Side fins and tail fins work like wings on an airplane. They help the shark go up, down, left, and right.

SHARK GILL SLITS

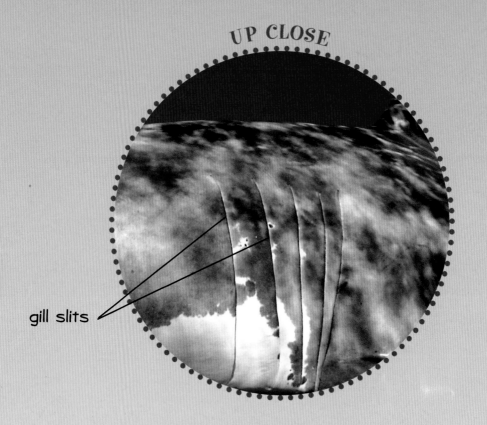

UP CLOSE

gill slits

Sharks do not breathe air. They get oxygen from the water. Water goes in the shark's mouth and out across the gills. Gills are inside the slits on the sides of the shark's head. Blood veins in the gills soak up oxygen.

water
out

water
in

SHARK PUPS

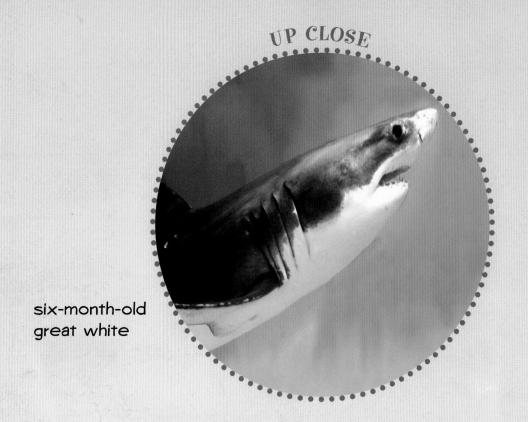

UP CLOSE

six-month-old
great white

A shark baby is called a pup. Two to twelve
pups are born at a time. Each gray-and-white
pup is about four feet long. As soon as they
are born, the pups swim away. They swim
and eat, swim and eat.

Soon they grow into huge hungry sharks.

LIFE CYCLE

Baby sharks are called pups. Two to twelve are born at a time.

Young sharks swim and eat, swim and eat.

Adult sharks grow to be about 20 feet long. They weigh almost 7,500 pounds.

22

LEARN MORE

BOOKS

Berger, Melvin. *What Do Sharks Eat for Dinner?* New York: Scholastic Reference, 2001.

Davies, Nicola. *Surprising Sharks.* Cambridge, Mass.: Candlewick Press, 2003.

MacQuitty, Miranda. *DK Eyewitness Books: Sharks.* New York: DK Children, 2004.

WEB SITES

Col, Jeananda. *Enchanted Learning.* © 1998–2005.
<http://www.enchantedlearning.com/subjects/sharks>

National Geographic Society.
National Geographic.com Kids. © 1996–2005.
<http://www.nationalgeographic.com/kids/index.html>
Click on "Creature Features." Then click on "Sharks."

INDEX

Series Literacy Consultant:
Allan A. De Fina, Ph.D.
Past President of the New Jersey Reading Association
Professor, Department of Literacy Education
New Jersey City University
Jersey City, New Jersey

Science Consultant:
Paul L. Sieswerda
Aquarium Curator
New York Aquarium
Brooklyn, New York

Note to Parents and Teachers: The **Zoom In on Animals!** series supports the National Science Education Standards for K–4 science. The Words to Know section introduces subject-specific vocabulary words, including pronunciation and definitions. Early readers may need help with these new words.

Library of Congress Cataloging-in-Publication Data

Bredeson, Carmen.
Great white sharks up close / Carmen Bredeson.
p. cm. — (Zoom in on animals!)
Includes index.
ISBN 0-7660-2495-4 (hardcover)
1. White shark—Juvenile literature. I. Title.
QL638.95.L3B74 2006
597.3'3—dc22
2005004989

Enslow Elementary
an imprint of
Enslow Publishers, Inc.
40 Industrial Road   PO Box 38
Box 398   Aldershot
Berkeley Heights, NJ 07922 Hants GU12 6BP
USA   UK
http://www.enslow.com

Printed in the United States of America

10 9 8 7 6 5 4 3 2 1

To Our Readers: We have done our best to make sure all Internet addresses in this book were active and appropriate when we went to press. However, the author and the publisher have no control over and assume no liability for the material available on those Internet sites or on other Web sites they may link to. Any comments or suggestions can be sent by e-mail to comments@enslow.com or to the address on the back cover.

Photo Credits: © 2004, Monteray Bay Aquarium Foundation, photography by Randy Wilder, pp. 20, 22 (top); © agefotostock/ SuperStock, pp. 11, 22 (middle); © Brandon Cole/Visuals Unlimited, p. 3; © Bruce Watkins/Animals Animals, p. 16; © Denis Scott/CORBIS, pp. 21, 22 (bottom); Eye of Science/Photo Researchers, Inc., p. 12; © James D. Watt/Norbert Wu Productions, www.norbertwu.com, p. 1; © James Watt/Animals Animals, p. 7, 9; © Marty Snyderman/Visuals Unlimited, pp. 14, 15; © OSF/Tobias Bernhard/Animals Animals, p. 13; © Phillip Colla/ www. oceanlight.com, pp. 17, 18, 19; Amos Nachoum/ Painet Inc., p. 10; David Fleetham/Painet Inc., pp. 4–5; Eric Haucke/ Greg Ochocki Productions/Photo Researchers, Inc., p. 8; Valerie Taylor/ardea.com, p. 6.

Cover Photos: © James D. Watt/Norbert Wu Productions, www.norbertwu.com, (left); Valerie Taylor/ardea.com (top right); Eye of Science/Photo Researchers, Inc., (middle right); © Bruce Watkins/ Animals Animals (bottom right).